P9-DCH-679

Naomi Osaka

CHERRY LAKE PRESS

Published in the United States of America by Cherry Lake Publishing
Ann Arbor, Michigan
www.cherrylakepublishing.com

Reading Adviser: Marla Conn, MS, Ed., Literacy specialist, Read-Ability, Inc.
Book Designer: Jennifer Wahi
Illustrator: Jeff Bane

Photo Credits: © Mirko Kuzmanovic/Shutterstock, 5; © Aleks_Shutter/Shutterstock, 7; © Viacheslav Nikolaenko/Shutterstock, 9; © Leonard Zhukovsky/Shutterstock, 11; © lev radin/Shutterstock, 13, 22; © Rena Schild/Shutterstock, 15, 23; © Jimmie48 Photography/Shutterstock, 17; © Contact1842/Dreamstime.com, 19; © action sports/Shutterstock, 21; Cover, 1, 6, 12, 18; Various frames throughout, © Shutterstock images

Cherry Lake Press is an imprint of Cherry Lake Publishing Group.

Library of Congress Cataloging-in-Publication Data

Names: Pincus, Meeg, author. | Bane, Jeff, 1957- illustrator.
Title: Naomi Osaka / Meeg Pincus ; illustrated by Jeff Bane.
Description: Ann Arbor, Michigan : Cherry Lake Publishing, 2021. | Series: My itty-bitty bio | Includes index. | Audience: Grades K-1
Identifiers: LCCN 2020005680 (print) | LCCN 2020005681 (ebook) | ISBN 9781534168381 (hardcover) | ISBN 9781534170063 (paperback) | ISBN 9781534171909 (pdf) | ISBN 9781534173743 (ebook)
Subjects: LCSH: Osaka, Naomi, 1997---Juvenile literature. | Women tennis players--United States--Biography--Juvenile literature. | Tennis players--United States--Biography--Juvenile literature.
Classification: LCC GV994.O73 P56 2021 (print) | LCC GV994.O73 (ebook) | DDC 796.342092 [B]--dc23
LC record available at https://lccn.loc.gov/2020005680
LC ebook record available at https://lccn.loc.gov/2020005681

Printed in the United States of America
Corporate Graphics

table of contents

About the author: Meeg Pincus has been a writer, editor, and educator for 25 years. She loves to write inspiring stories for kids about people, animals, and our planet. She lives near San Diego, California, where she enjoys the beach, reading, singing, and her family.

About the illustrator: Jeff Bane and his two business partners own a studio along the American River in Folsom, California, home of the 1849 Gold Rush. When Jeff's not sketching or illustrating for clients, he's either swimming or kayaking in the river to relax.

I was born in Osaka, Japan. It was 1997.

I have an older sister.

My parents are **immigrants**. My mother is from Japan. My father is from Haiti. We moved to the United States when I was 3.

Where is your family from?

My sister and I loved tennis growing up. Our dad coached us. Our mom earned money so we could **compete**. Our parents supported our dream of becoming great players.

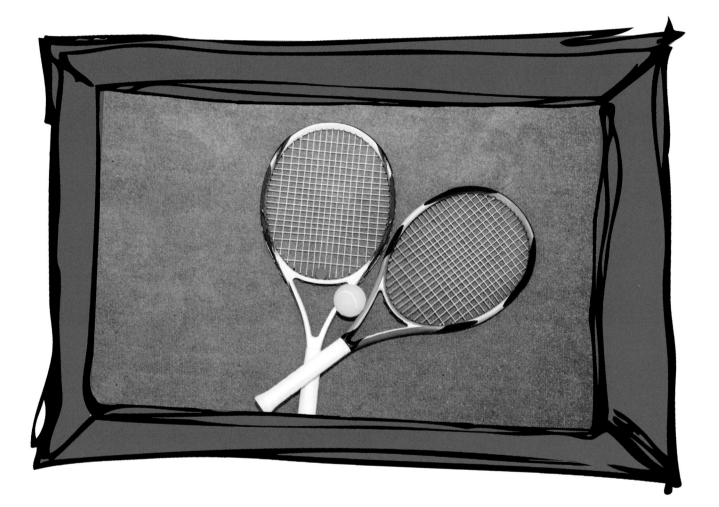

I looked up to Serena Williams. She was my **idol**. I dreamed of playing against her.

What do you dream of doing?

I became a **professional** tennis player at age 16. I played against Serena Williams. I won!

I became the world's top
women's tennis player. I was 21.

I respect my **opponents**. People say I am a **good sport**.

What makes a good sport?

I like to travel. I play tennis for Japan. I live in the United States. I visit Haiti. My parents built a school there.

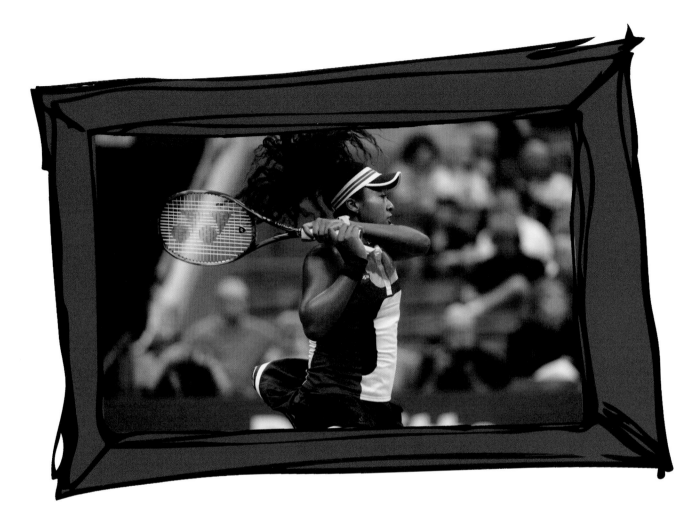

I am proud to be Japanese, Haitian, and American. I am proud to play tennis. I am proud to be kind.

What would you like to ask me?

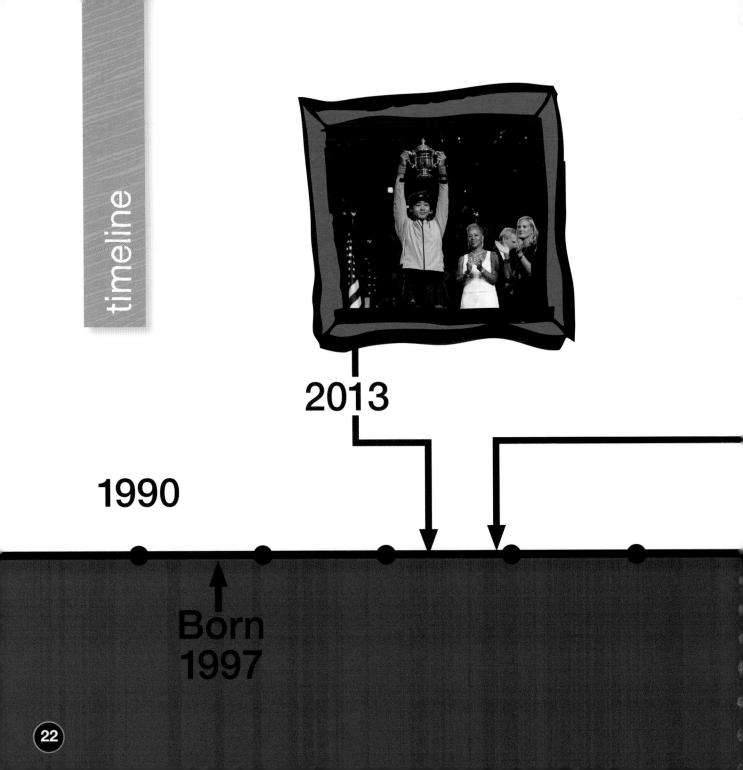

timeline

2013

1990

↑
Born
1997

22

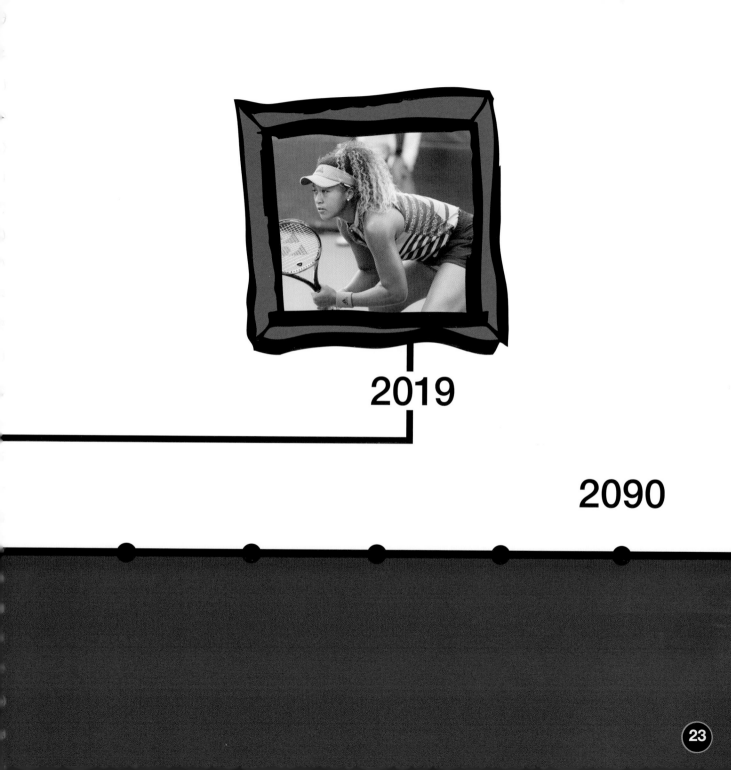

2019

2090

glossary

compete (kuhm-PEET) to try hard to outdo others in a contest, game, or task

good sport (GUD SPORT) a person who plays fair and accepts winning or losing with good manners

idol (EYE-duhl) a popular person admired and loved for their accomplishments

immigrants (IM-ih-gruhnts) people who move from one country to another and settle there

opponents (uh-POH-nuhnts) the people or teams you play or compete against in games or contests

professional (pruh-FESH-uh-nuhl) making money for working hard at something others do for fun

index